For my son Bennett, who inspires me every day
—AW

For all the noodle lovers
—KU

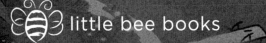

New York, NY | Text copyright © 2019 by Andrea Wang | Illustrations copyright © 2019 by Kana Urbanowicz | All rights reserved, including the right of reproduction in whole or in part in any form. | Manufactured in Thailand RRD 0722 | 15 14 13 12 11 10 9

Library of Congress Cataloging-in-Publication Data
Names: Wang, Andrea, author. | Urbanowicz, Kana, illustrator. | Title: Magic ramen / by Andrea Wang; illustrated by Kana Urbanowicz.
Description: First edition. | New York, NY: Little Bee Books, [2019] | "Every day, Ando Momofuku would retire to his lab—a little shed in his backyard. For years, he'd dreamed about making a new kind of ramen noodle soup that was quick, convenient, and tasty to feed the hungry people he'd seen in line for a bowl on the black market following World War II. "Peace follows from a full stomach," he believed. Day after day, Ando experimented. Night after night, he failed. But Ando kept experimenting. With persistence, creativity, and a little inspiration, Ando succeeded. This is the true story behind one of the world's most popular foods"—Provided by publisher. | Includes bibliographical references. | Audience: Ages 4–8. Audience: K to grade 3. | Identifiers: LCCN 2018007582 | Subjects: LCSH: Ramen—Japan—History—Juvenile literature. | Ando, Momofuku, 1910–2007—Juvenile literature.
Classification: LCC TX809.N65 W36 2019 | DDC 641.82/2—dc23
LC record available at https://lccn.loc.gov/2018007582

ISBN: 978-1-4998-0703-5
littlebeebooks.com
For more information about special discounts on bulk purchases, please contact Little Bee Books at sales@littlebeebooks.com

MAGIC RAMEN

THE STORY OF
MOMOFUKU ANDO

WRITTEN BY
ANDREA WANG

ILLUSTRATED BY
KANA URBANOWICZ

little bee books

Momofuku Ando picked his way through the rubble on his way home from work.

Even though World War II had ended over a year ago, much of Osaka, Japan, still lay in ruins.

Across the street, a long line of people wound down the sidewalk.
It was winter and they shivered in their ragged clothes.

What are they waiting for?
Ando wondered.

At the head of the line, billows of steam rose from
a shack. Inside, a man was selling ramen noodle soup.

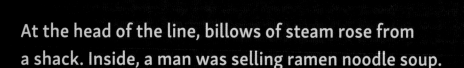

Bad harvests, rationing, and war had made food scarce.
The poor ate grass and bark to survive. Orphans scrounged through
garbage for something to eat. Those lucky enough to have some money
waited for hours and paid outrageous prices for a meager bowl of ramen.

Ando went home, but he couldn't forget the hungry people. *The world is peaceful only when everyone has enough to eat,* he realized. Ando decided that food would be his life's work.

He started a business making salt. He caught and dried fish. He created nutritious food for people who were sick. With every new product, every new job, and every new business, Ando thought about the line of starving people. He thought about them for over ten years. Then, one of Ando's business deals ended badly. He was penniless. Once again, Ando remembered the thin and hungry people.

Wouldn't it be wonderful, he thought, *if whole families could have noodles whenever they wanted?* No more waiting in line in the cold. No more high prices. No more empty stomachs.

He dreamed about a new kind of ramen. His ramen wouldn't be like other noodles. It would be more nutritious. In a shed in his backyard, Ando mixed flour, salt, and water together.

He added eggs.

He added powdered milk.

He even added spinach!

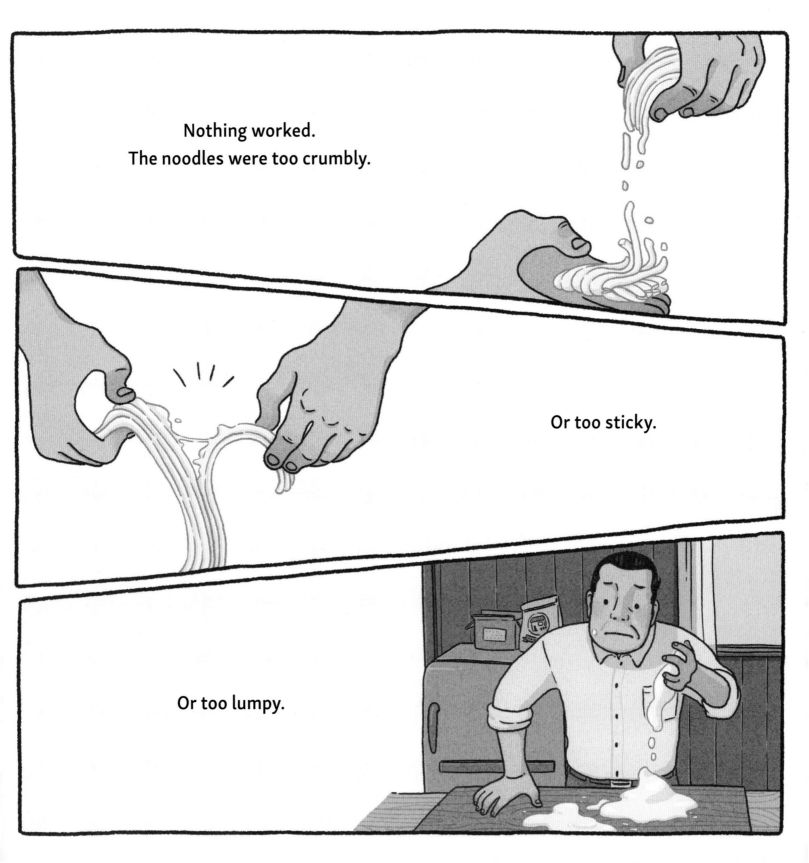

Nothing worked.
The noodles were too crumbly.

Or too sticky.

Or too lumpy.

Ando kept experimenting with different ingredients.

One day, he cranked the handle of his noodle-making machine and tested the noodles that came out.

They didn't crumble, stick, or lump. It was just the right mix of ingredients.

Ando realized, *The key to the preparation of food is balance.*

But what was ramen without soup?
Ando remembered the cold and hungry people.
Chicken soup warmed up cold bodies but took hours to make.

His ramen would be tasty and easy to cook. The simple addition of hot water would release flavor from the noodles and turn it into hot chicken soup.

Ando kept experimenting.

He used chicken soup to make the dough.

He brushed seasonings onto the noodles.

He dipped the noodles into soup.

Once again, nothing worked.

The noodles were too brittle.

Or too soft.

Or too soggy.

Ando kept experimenting with different methods.

One day, he sprinkled noodles with soup from a watering can,
then tossed and separated them.

The noodles soaked up the soup and dried. It was just the right procedure.

He added hot water to the dried noodles and stirred. The water now tasted like soup!

But the noodles were too tough. They still had to be cooked on a stove.

Ando remembered the tired and hungry people. He wanted his ramen to be fast and convenient. It could be made with hot water and in a few minutes. People should be able to make it "anywhere, anytime."

Day after day, Ando experimented.
Night after night, he failed.
Month after month, he kept trying.
Nothing worked.

One night, Ando watched his wife, Masako, fry tempura.

She coated vegetables and seafood in batter and dropped them into hot oil. The water in the batter evaporated and left tiny holes in the now-crunchy coating.

He stared at the tempura.
The batter was made from flour and
water—just like his noodles. . . .

"Yatta!" he cried. "That's it!"
He raced to his shed and threw
some noodles into a pot of hot oil.

They sizzled.

And popped.

And crisped.

Ando scooped the fried noodles out of the oil and into a bowl. He added hot water and waited. The water seeped into the tiny holes and softened the noodles.

Two minutes later, he plunged a pair of chopsticks into the bowl. He stirred and slurped. The noodles were tender and chewy. They floated in a bowl of hot and tasty soup.

Ando worked hard to make enough instant ramen to sell. The whole family pitched in: Masako, Suma, Koki, and even little Akemi.

Ando gave demonstrations.
He poured hot water.

He waited two minutes.

"*Mahō no ramen!*"
the astonished
customers
exclaimed.
"Magic ramen!"

Soon, everyone was eating Ando's ramen.

Poor people.

Children.

Busy workers.

Even royalty!

Ando's ramen was nutritious, tasty, and convenient. Thin, cold, tired, and hungry people ate it and felt better.

Ando smiled. "Peace follows from a full stomach," he said. Ever since, Momofuku Ando and his backyard invention have fostered peace, one bowl of noodles at a time.

AUTHOR'S NOTE

In this book, we follow the Western custom of presenting a person's full name with the given name (first name) followed by the surname (family name). For Momofuku Ando, his given name is Momofuku and his surname is Ando. Why is he referred to as Ando throughout the story? In Japan, most people are called by their surnames. First names are usually only used for children and among family members and close friends.

PRONUNCIATION GUIDE

Akemi: AH-keh-mee

Ando: AHN-doh

Koki: KOH-kee

mahō no ramen: mah-HO no RAH-men

Masako: MAH-sah-koh

Momofuku: MOH-moh-foo-koo

Osaka: OH-sah-kah

ramen: RAH-men

Suma: SUE-mah

tempura: TEM-poo-rah

yatta: YAH-tah

AFTERWORD

When Momofuku Ando saw the long lines of starving people, he saw a need, one he was inspired to fill. For years, he dreamed about making new food that would nourish people and help ease their suffering. Thanks to his creative thinking and persistence, Ando's dream came true. In 1958, twelve years after seeing hungry people at the black market ramen stall, he invented Chikin Ramen, the first instant ramen.

Born in Taiwan in 1910, Ando immigrated to Japan as a young man and embraced his adopted country. In postwar Japan, his instant ramen provided valuable nutrients and calories to hungry people. At first, instant ramen was not a huge hit. The price of Chikin Ramen was higher than a bowl of fresh noodles. But people loved how fast and easy it was to make. Soon, prices fell as it became more popular. Ando's company, Nissin Foods, now sells instant ramen all over the world. They also supply millions of packages of instant ramen to other countries to feed the poor and those left homeless through earthquakes, hurricanes, wars, and other calamities.

Ando continued to find new ways to make instant ramen more nutritious. He added an indentation on the top of Chikin Ramen noodles so an egg could be easily poached at the same time the noodles cooked. He also added vitamins and freeze-dried vegetables. Recently, Nissin improved their recipes by reducing and/or replacing salt, artificial flavors, and MSG, a preservative.

Throughout his life, Ando also continued to invent. He created Cup Noodles, which could be made right in its own container—no bowl needed! Even at the age of 91, Ando invented Space Ram, instant noodles that could be eaten in zero gravity. In 2005, two years before Ando's death, Japanese astronaut Soichi Noguchi became the first person to eat ramen in outer space, aboard the US space shuttle *Discovery*.

Ando's instant ramen is not only magic, it's out of this world!

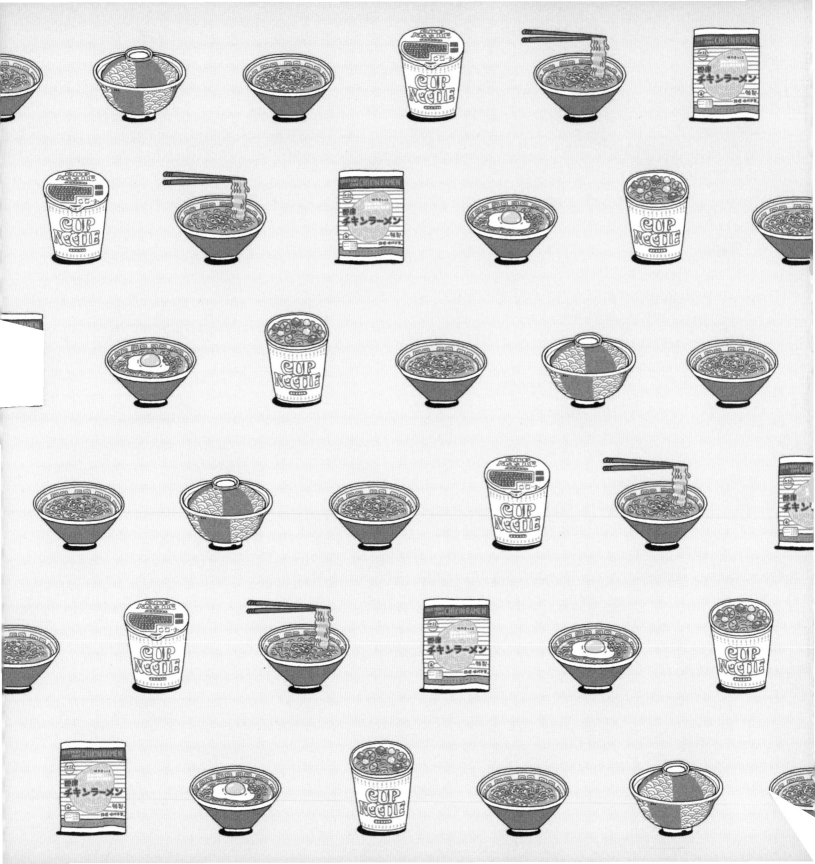